Letts

Framework FOCUS

YEAR 7

Spelling

Louis Fidge
Ray Barker

How to use this book

Letts Framework Focus: Spelling books have been designed to provide a versatile resource, capable of being used for a variety of teaching and learning situations and by a wide range of teachers – specialists and non-specialists alike. They:

- contain 30 units of work, sufficient for one school year
- are straightforward and easy to use
- provide discrete double-page spread format for quick reference
- have a clear teaching focus
- contain differentiated activities for each objective.

Letts Framework Focus: Spelling books can be used in a variety of ways:

- They easily provide work for the whole class, groups or individuals.
- Use them to introduce a key literacy topic – as a lesson 'starter'.
- The structure of the pages allows for teaching a particular literacy issue to the whole class.
- Units allow teachers to focus on a particular issue if this seems a problem for an individual or group.
- Planned progression allows teachers to consolidate, develop and extend literacy work over the year.
- Each unit provides work for follow-up homework assignments.

As a lesson starter

The Spelling Focus provides a clear explanation of each objective with examples for discussion or illustration. Appropriate activities may be chosen from the range of differentiated tasks for discussion, or to work through with the class.

Group and individual work

These books are ideal for group and individual work. Teaching on the same subject can be realistically matched appropriately to individual pupils' abilities, allowing pupils to work independently.

Homework

The design of the material in the books provides an ideal solution to meaningful homework assignments – differentiated appropriately for each pupil.

Contents Year 7 Spelling

Unit 1: Vowel sounds

Objectives

- To consolidate and secure correct vowel choices.
- To explore the differences between the vowel sounds 'a' and 'o', especially in 'wa' and 'wo' words.

Spelling Focus

- The alphabet contains **five** letters that are called **vowels**. All the other letters in the alphabet are called **consonants**.
- As a rule, all words contain **at least one vowel** – or sometimes a 'y'.
- The letters 'a' and 'o' are often pronounced differently after the letter 'w'.

The wonderful wolf played with the wobbling top.

- Sometimes the sounds produced by these vowels can cause problems:

In ***'wash'*** the letter ***'a'*** is pronounced like ***'o'***.

In ***'wonderful'*** the letter ***'o'*** can be pronounced in a variety of ways.

In ***'swarm'*** the letters ***'ar'*** are pronounced like ***'or'***.

In ***'world'*** the letters ***'or'*** are pronounced like ***'er'***.

vowel box

a
e
i
o
u

Starter

1. Copy the words below. Complete each word with an 'a' or an 'o'. Check your answers in a dictionary.

(a) w _ nt
(b) w _ s
(c) w _ sh
(d) w _ nder
(e) w _ sp
(f) w _ llet
(g) w _ ddle
(h) w _ d
(i) sw _ n
(j) sw _ mp
(k) sw _ llow

2. Copy and complete the chart. Describe what sounds each of these vowels makes in the words above. Note down other words that make the same sound, if there are any.

Original word	Sound made	Example
wasp	*almost an 'o'*	*want*

Practice >>

3 Copy the words below. Write a definition for each word. Use a dictionary.

(a) wobble
(b) wombat
(c) won
(d) wonderful
(e) worry
(f) wolf
(g) womb
(h) woman

4 How many different ways is the letter 'o' pronounced in the words above? Copy out the chart below and write the words in sets according to their sounds. One has been done for you.

Sounds like a *'u'* in *'son'*		
worry		

Extension >>>

5 Copy these words. Choose 'ar' or 'or' to complete each word.

(a) w _ _ k
(b) rew _ _ d
(c) sw _ _ m
(d) w _ _ thy
(e) w _ _ th
(f) w _ _ rant
(g) w _ _ p
(h) w _ _ e
(i) dw _ _ f
(j) w _ _ m
(k) w _ _ d
(l) w _ _ n

6 Which words can take both 'ar' and 'or'?

7 What do you notice about the way 'ar' and 'or' are pronounced in the words you have made?

8 Write five words beginning with 'w' in each column to complete the chart.

Phoneme 'ai'	Phoneme 'oo'	Phoneme 'ou'
waist	*wood*	*wound*

9 Which words make completely different vowel sounds?

REMEMBER

A phoneme is the smallest unit of sound in a word.

Feedback

Do vowels always make the sound they make in the alphabet? For instance, ***'ant'*** has a different ***'a'*** sound from ***'ace'***. Your job is to investigate words to find out what makes the difference, for example, does ***'a'*** always sound 'long' before a ***'ce'***? Do double vowels make different sounds from single ones? Note examples and exceptions as you learn something new.

Unit 2: Unstressed vowels

Objectives

- To consolidate and secure correct vowel choices.
- To spell unstressed vowels in polysyllabic words.

Spelling Focus

- A **polysyllabic** word is a word with more than one syllable. 'Poly' means 'more than one'.
- Sometimes, vowels in these words are not 'stressed' or pronounced and so they become difficult to spell. For example:

  'temperature' is often pronounced

  'temprature'.

  A good way to deal with this is to break words into syllables.

vowel box

a
e
i
o
u

Starter

1 Join up the syllables in each sum and write the word. Write the number of syllables in brackets after the word.
com + pu + ter = computer (3)

(a) some + thing =
(b) sta + tion + ary =
(c) com + pa + ny =
(d) Sat + ur + day =
(e) tem + per + at + ure =
(f) im + por + tant =
(g) thes + au + rus =

Circle any vowels you think may be unstressed in the words you made.

2 Now divide these commonly misspelled words into syllables by yourself. Do it like this:
Something = some + thing (2)
Remember that each syllable must contain a vowel.

(a) abandoned
(b) astronomy
(c) benefit
(d) category
(e) consonant
(f) definite

Underline the vowels which you think will be unstressed.

Practice >>

3 Copy the words. Write in the missing vowels.

- (a) t _ rr _ f _ c
- (b) b _ _ _ t _ f _ l
- (c) c _ mp _ ny
- (d) _ nt _ r _ st _ ng
- (e) d _ ff _ r _ nt
- (f) p _ _ s _ n _ _ s
- (g) st _ t _ _ n _ ry
- (h) p _ rt _ bl _
- (i) c _ rp _ t
- (j) fr _ _ d _ m
- (k) _ xtr _ _ rd _ n _ ry

4 Break up the words into syllables, using a slash (/) to separate each syllable.

5 Circle the vowels which you think are unstressed.

Extension >>>

6 Copy and complete the chart. This will show how the structure and derivation of words can help you to spell them. Note that sometimes the spelling of the root word is changed slightly. Use these words:
signature, celebration, temperature, independence, description

Word root	Prefix	Suffix
sign	*X*	*-ature*

REMEMBER
Use the Look, Say, Cover, Write, Check spelling strategy to help you.

7 Write mnemonics which would help you spell these words, using the clues in brackets.
There's a RAT in separate.

- (a) temperature (temper)
- (b) company (pan)
- (c) practice (ice)
- (d) interesting (rest)
- (e) extraordinary (extra)

Feedback

Try breaking words into syllables and sounding out each one. You will see how words are composed of separate parts. Invent mnemonics to help you remember words.

There's a hot TEMPER in temperature.

Look for root words and see if the derivation of words will help.

Unit 3: Consonants and syllables

Objectives

- To sound out words phonemically and by syllables.
- To spell two-syllable words containing double consonants.

Spelling Focus

- **Consonants** are the **21 letters** of the alphabet that are **not vowels** (a, e, i, o, u).
- We can break down words into **smaller parts** called **syllables**.
- In two-syllable words containing a **double** consonant, we make the syllable break **between** the two consonants.

ten / nis, Den / nis

- When we extend single-syllable words with one vowel before the final consonant, we usually double the final consonant.

sun → *sunny*

Starter

1 Write the words below and circle the double consonant in each.

(a) dripping
(b) swimmer
(c) rubbish
(d) fatten
(e) chatty
(f) thinnest
(g) wagging
(h) beggar
(i) happy
(j) supply
(k) sudden
(l) marry

2 Split the words according to the number of syllables.
Do it like this:

shop+ping = shopping (2)

3 Which of the words above have recognisable roots?
For example: *shopping – shop*.

4 Check the spelling of these words in a dictionary.
Write the correct versions.

(a) writen/written
(b) training/traning
(c) fiter/fitter
(d) beeping/beepping

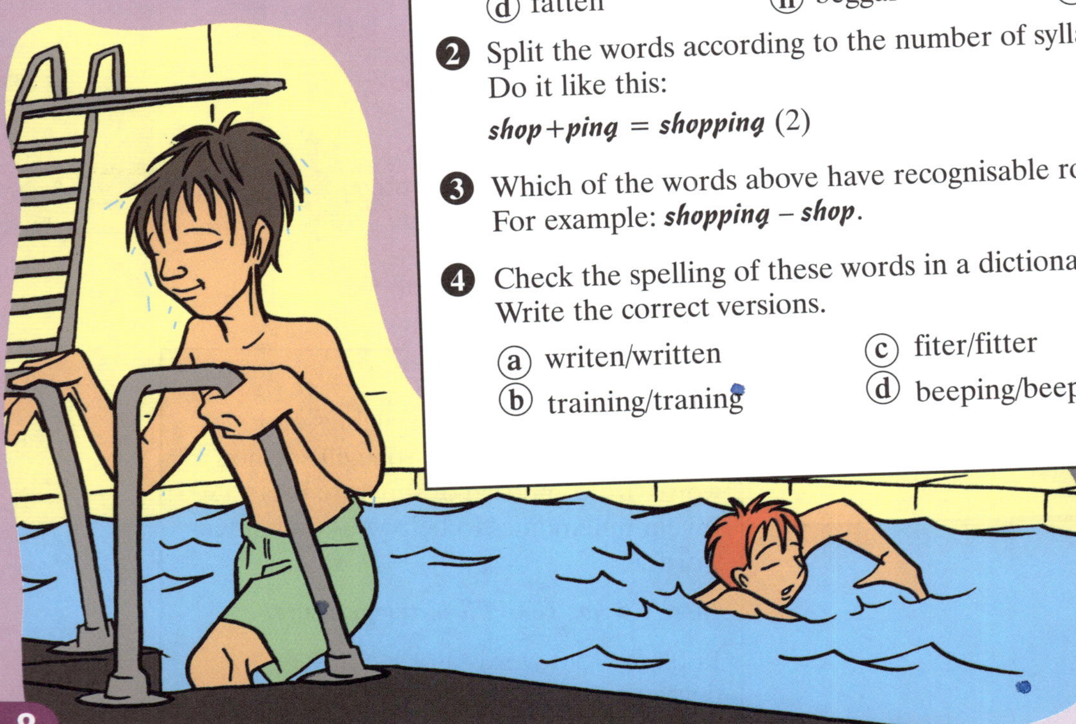

Practice >>

5 Find all the two-syllable words containing a double consonant in the box. Split the words into syllables and write them out.

runner	*offend*	*curry*
ugly	*hungry*	*intend*
label	*transparent*	*kingdom*
photograph	*smuggler*	*pillow*
attempt	*hollow*	*newspaper*
puppet	*rabbit*	*poem*
disgusting	*clammy*	*dictionary*
tunnel	*spider*	*lantern*

Extension >>>

6 Copy the words below. Think of a double consonant to complete each word. Check your answers in a dictionary.

(a) co _ _ ect
(b) fu _ _ el
(c) fo _ _ ow
(d) pa _ _ age
(e) bu _ _ on
(f) ca _ _ age
(g) a _ _ oy
(h) su _ _ ess
(i) sto _ _ er
(j) o _ _ end
(k) su _ _ est
(l) sni _ _ le
(m) sa _ _ le
(n) no _ _ le
(o) pu _ _ ing

7 Now write each word again, splitting it into syllables.

Feedback

Double letters often cause difficulties in spelling. Splitting words into syllables can help you to decide which words contain them. Learning and practising rules, such as those in the Spelling Focus, will also help.

Use a dictionary to check your spelling if you are in doubt.

Unit 4: Doubling consonants

Objectives

- To consolidate and secure the influence of vowels on other letters.
- To explore spelling patterns of consonants and formulate rules.

Spelling Focus

- Letters can be divided into **vowels** and **consonants**. The vowels are a, e, i, o, u. The rest of the letters are consonants.
- When you word build by adding **suffixes** such as '**ing**' and '**ed**' to words, **sometimes** the **final consonant doubles**.

  stop - stopping - stopped; hop - hopping - hopped

  This does not happen in words such as ***hope - hoping***.
- When adding suffixes such as 'ing' and 'ed' to single syllable words ending in a consonant which is preceded by one vowel, the last letter is doubled.
- When adding 'ing' or 'ed' to words ending in 'e', drop the final 'e' otherwise the combination of the two vowels would make a completely different sound.

Starter

1 Copy and complete the chart.

Root words	+ing	+ed
(a) *rob*	*robbing*	*robbed*
(b) *shop*		
(c) *beg*		
(d) *hop*		
(e) *pin*		
(f) *sip*		
(g) *sin*		

Use a dictionary to check your spelling.

Practice >>

2 Add 'ing' to the words in the box. Check your spelling in a dictionary.

shop	cry	hope	skip	hum
cool	run	dig	hop	fume
win	get	fail	feel	tap

3 Copy and complete the chart using the words in the box above.

Word	No. of syllables	Last letter	Second to last letter	Third to last letter
shop	1	consonant	vowel	consonant

4 Look at your answers to question 2 and find the words which doubled their final consonants. Now find these words in your chart. Do you notice anything that they all have in common?

Extension >>>

5 Complete this sentence to give a useful spelling rule.

When you add a suffix such as ____ and ____ to single-syllable words which end in ______________________, then the final consonant ________________.

6 Can you find any exceptions to the rule?

7 Make more words by adding 'er' and 'ed' if possible to the words in (2) above.

Explain whether they follow the same rule.

8 Write sentences using five of your new words.

Feedback

There are two spelling rules to help you add 'ing' and 'ed' to words. You need to be able to identify a syllable, a vowel and a consonant.

- With single-syllable words ending in a vowel then a consonant, we double the consonant before adding the suffix.

  shop ⟶ *shopping*

- With single-syllable words ending in a consonant then 'e', we drop the 'e' before adding the suffix.

  mope ⟶ *moping*

Unit 5: Soft and hard letters

Objectives

- To revise the influence of vowels on other letters.
- To explore spelling patterns of consonants and formulate rules.

Spelling Focus

- Letters can be divided into vowels and consonants. The vowels are a, e, i, o, u. The rest of the letters are consonants.
- Some consonants are pronounced in a 'hard' way. For example, the 'c' in 'cat' and the 'g' in 'get' sound 'hard'.
- The same consonants can be pronounced in a 'soft' way. For example, the 'c' in 'pace' and the 'g' in 'general' sound 'soft'.

Starter

1 Pronounce each of the following words. Decide whether the 'c' is hard (h) or soft (s). The first one has been done for you.

camera (h)	*celebrate*	*cobweb*	*coffin*
accident	*discuss*	*centimetre*	*cupboard*
cinnamon	*census*	*cereal*	

2 Copy the words. Circle the 'c' or 'g' consonant in each word. Write by the word if they sound 'hard' or 'soft'. The first one is done for you.

Circle	soft/ hard	Circle	soft/ hard	Circle	soft/ hard
great	hard	*manager*		*gift*	
cellar		*cupboard*		*centre*	
disguise		*change*		*damage*	
cord		*notice*		*rice*	
ceiling		*guess*		*coal*	
goalkeeper		*content*			
cottage		*ranger*			

Practice >>

3 Look at the 'c' words below.

card	circle	cement	content	cat
custard	France	pencil	city	come
record	cabbage	cut	cell	cup

Put the 'c' words in the correct columns below, according to which vowel comes after the 'c'. What do you notice about the sounds of the 'c' words in each column?

a	e	i	o	u
card				

4 Look at the 'g' words below.

gasp	gem	gulf	gate	giraffe
guitar	gape	gone	general	tongue
gin	gold	damage	god	giant

Put the 'g' words in the correct columns below, according to which vowel comes after the 'g'. What do you notice about the sounds of the 'g' words in each column?

a	e	i	o	u
gasp				

Extension >>>

5 Copy and complete these rules about when 'c' and 'g' are hard or soft:

(a) *The letter 'c' is pronounced soft if it appears before ...*
(b) *Before other vowels 'c' is ...*
(c) *The letter 'g' is pronounced soft if it appears before ...*
Before other vowels 'g' is ...

6 Use a dictionary to find:

(a) three more examples to prove the rules given above
(b) three exceptions to any of the rules, e.g. gift, get.

Write five sentences using some of your new words.

Feedback

After you have investigated the spelling of these words, you should be in a position to produce some rules that will help you to remember how to spell words containing hard and soft 'g' and 'c' consonants.

Remember the simple way of learning how to spell difficult words: LOOK, SAY, COVER, WRITE, CHECK.

Unit 6: Plurals

Objective

- To investigate what happens to words ending in 'f' when they are suffixed.

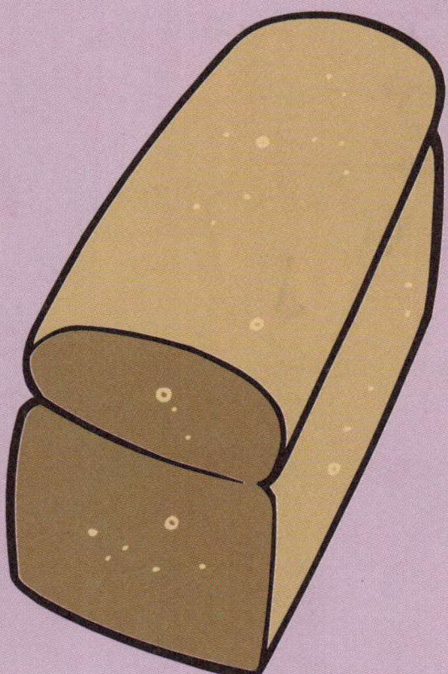

Spelling Focus

- When a noun ends in 'f' or 'fe', we usually change the 'f' to 'v' and add 'es' when we write it in the plural.

one loaf, two loaves

- Note that a few nouns ending in 'f' do not follow this rule. They just add 's' in the plural.

chiefs

roofs

handkerchiefs

waifs

gulfs

Starter

1 Copy and complete this chart.

Singular	Plural
leaf	*leaves*
loaf	
calf	
	halves
thief	
	elves
shelf	
	scarves
wolf	

Think of five more nouns in the singular that end in 'f'. Write their plurals. Do they all follow the rule?

2 Check the correct spellings of these words in a dictionary.

cuf/cuff; staff/staf; snif/sniff; stuf/stuff; clif/cliff; bluf/bluff

How are their plurals made?

Practice >>

3 Write the singular form of each of these nouns.

(a) thieves
(b) sheaves
(c) calves
(d) wives
(e) knives
(f) lives
(g) loaves
(h) shelves

4 Write the plural form of each of these nouns. Check your answers in a dictionary. What do you notice?

(a) self
(b) leaf
(c) wife
(d) chief
(e) hoof
(f) wolf
(g) half
(h) waif

Extension >>>

5 Copy these sentences. Use the plural form of a noun ending in 'f' to fill each gap.

(a) You need sharp __________ to cut tough meat.
(b) The baker laid out the freshly-baked __________.
(c) In autumn, many trees drop their __________.
(d) The cow gave birth to two __________.
(e) The __________ in the shop were laden with chocolates.
(f) A cat is said to have nine __________.
(g) The pack of __________ roamed the forest.
(h) A man who has two __________ is called a bigamist.
(i) The cake was cut into equal __________.
(j) Two __________ broke into the bank and stole the money.

REMEMBER

Plurals can be awkward. Following any rules is helpful.

Feedback

There are other rules for deciding how to make the plurals of words.

Consider words ending in 'y'. When do you add an 's' or 'ies'? Look at these two words:

monkey – monkeys

baby – babies

Devise a rule of your own. Find other examples to back up your investigation.

Unit 7: Growing words

Objective

- To practise extending and compounding words through adding parts.

Spelling Focus

- We can make some words longer by adding a **prefix** at the **beginning** or a **suffix** at the **end**.

  This sometimes has an impact on spelling.

  'Happy' is a root word.

  We can add a negative prefix ***'un'*** to make the opposite ***'unhappy'***.

  The spelling of the root word does not change.

  We can add the suffix ***'ness'*** to make an abstract noun ***'happiness'***.

  Notice how the root word changes spelling: the ***'y'*** changes to ***'i'***.

Starter

1. Copy the words below.
   Choose from the prefixes 'un' or 'dis' to fill each gap.
   (a) __ agree
   (b) __ trust
   (c) __ dress
   (d) __ do
   (e) __ obey
   (f) __ fair
   Check your answers in a dictionary.

2. Copy the words below.
   Choose from the prefixes 're' or 'de' to fill each gap.
   (a) __ place
   (b) __ parted
   (c) __ form
   (d) __ trace
   (e) __ face
   (f) __ call
   Check your answers in a dictionary.
   Which words can take both?

3. Does the spelling of the root word change when a prefix is added?
   How does each prefix affect the meaning of words?

REMEMBER

Negative prefixes do not change the spelling of the root word.

Practice >>

4 Copy these words. Then write each word without its suffix.
Do it like this: ***crunchy = crunch + y***
Note that sometimes the spelling of root words might change slightly.

(a) funnily (b) noisy (c) starry (d) older (e) bravest (f) heavier (g) merciful (h) pitiless (i) simply (j) angrily (k) artist (l) drummer

5 Give these words the opposite meaning by changing the suffix.

(a) hopeful (b) powerful (c) useful (d) harmless (e) colourless (f) thankless (g) merciless

6 What do you notice about the spelling of the suffix when you want to suggest that a word is 'full' of something?

Extension >>>

7 Extend each word below by adding a prefix.
Do it like this: ***dress – undress***
Check your answers in a dictionary.

(a) behave (b) port (c) obey (d) order (e) calculate (f) hale (g) caution (h) posit

8 Extend each word below by adding a suffix.
Do it like this: ***slow – slowly***
Check your answers in a dictionary.

(a) fault (b) empty (c) nice (d) miserable (e) hungry (f) call (g) act (h) swim

9 Extend each of the following words by adding a prefix and a suffix to it.
Do it like this: ***help – unhelpful***
Check your answers in a dictionary.

(a) happy (b) vent (c) judge (d) stand (e) cover (f) turn (g) count (h) health

Feedback

A useful way of learning how to spell words is to look at the component parts of words. Many words have a 'root' which you can build upon with suffixes (word endings) and prefixes (word beginnings).

Unit 8: Suffixes

Objective

- To consolidate and secure building up spellings using known suffixes.

Spelling Focus

- A **suffix** is a **group of letters** added to the **end** of a word to **change its meaning**.

  Soft can become ***softness***, ***softly*** or ***soften***.

- Sometimes you can recognise ancient Greek or Latin suffixes which mean something quite specific. For example:

  '***graph***' *or* '***graphy***' comes from an ancient Greek word meaning 'to write about'.

  'geo-graphy' is the study of (writings about) the earth (geo).

Starter

1. Write out the words and underline the suffix in each example.
   (a) advertisement, encouragement, movement
   (b) washable, breakable, portable
   (c) accidental, musical, national
   (d) dirty, watery, angry
   (e) childish, foolish, girlish
   (f) girlhood, boyhood, childhood
   (g) shopping, hoping, crashing
2. Write the root word to which the suffix has been added.
3. The suffix 'ing' is a 'vowel suffix' because it starts with a vowel. Think of four more vowel suffixes and find examples of words ending in them.
   Examine what happens when these suffixes are added to a word.
   Do they change the spelling of the root word?

Practice >>

4 Look at the box below.

en	*ish*	*ed*	*ing*	*al*	*et*
er	*able*	*ive*	*est*	*y*	*ous*

Add suffixes from the box to the words below to make as many new words as you can.

For example: ***hop – hopped – hopping***

Check your answers in a dictionary.

- (a) hop
- (b) shop
- (c) big
- (d) swim
- (e) scan
- (f) skip
- (g) fun
- (h) rub
- (i) clap
- (j) win
- (k) clean
- (l) pat
- (m) wag
- (n) wet
- (o) fat
- (p) thin
- (q) cook
- (r) pin
- (s) skin
- (t) chop
- (u) chat
- (v) blot

5 Underline the words you have made which double their last consonant when you add a suffix. Make up a rule for these words.

Extension >>>

6 The suffix 'cide' comes from Latin and means 'to cut' or 'to kill', so insecticide is something that kills insects. Match each word in the box with a meaning and write your answers. Use your dictionary to help.

homicide	*suicide*	*regicide*	*matricide*	*infanticide*

- (a) killing yourself
- (b) killing a child
- (c) killing your mother
- (d) killing the King
- (e) killing anybody

7 The suffix 'ology' comes from Ancient Greek. Copy and complete the puzzle with three more 'ology' words. Find out what the suffix means.

- (a) psych ology
- (b) ______ ology
- (c) ______ ology
- (d) ______ ology

Feedback

You need to be able to separate the root of a word from its suffix. Adding certain suffixes to words can change the spelling of the root word.

In single-syllable words with one vowel before the final consonant, the consonant will double when most suffixes are added.

Unit 9: Past tenses

Objectives

- To consolidate and secure word endings.
- To spell irregular tense changes.

Spelling Focus

- The **past tense** of many regular verbs is written as you would expect.

  I jump the fence.

  I jumped the fence.

- The past tense of some verbs is not always written as you would expect. We call these verbs **irregular**.

  I go to secondary school.

  I went to primary school.

  I never think about school.

  I never thought about school.

Starter

1 Match up the present and the past tenses of these verbs. Write them like this: *drink – drank*

Present tense (Today I …)	Past tense (Yesterday I …)
drink	*broke*
am	*grew*
break	*drank*
wear	*taught*
think	*was*
shake	*did*
grow	*thought*
do	*left*
leave	*wore*
teach	*shook*

2 Copy and complete this chart with the past tense of the verbs.

Present tense (Today I …)	Past tense (Yesterday I …)
write	*wrote*
sit	
take	
sink	
have	
make	
get	

Practice >>

3 Copy these sentences. Complete them by using the past tense of the verb in brackets.

(a) The man _____ the bell. (ring)
(b) I _____ in a whisper. (speak)
(c) The children _____ their bikes to the shops. (ride)
(d) The child _____ an awful picture of the teacher. (draw)
(e) The lion _____ from behind a bush. (spring)
(f) Edward never _____ all his school meals. (eat)
(g) We _____ many different kinds of animals at the theme park. (see)
(h) The water _____ in the pond last winter. (freeze)

Extension >>>

4 Identify the verbs in these sentences. Rewrite the sentences, changing the verbs into the past tense.

(a) I rise early and choose the trainers to wear.
(b) I get dressed and take my book downstairs.
(c) We give the dog a bone and he bites it.
(d) My mum catches the bus to work.
(e) The child falls over and breaks a leg.
(f) The clock strikes twelve as the boy leaves.
(g) We always sing a song as we ride our bikes.
(h) My sister goes to the party and wears a fantastic designer outfit.

REMEMBER

The tense of a verb tells you when the action takes place.

Feedback

Changing the tense of a verb often makes a change in the spelling of the verb.

Many verbs follow a pattern when they change tense – they are regular. However, many verbs are irregular.

Some of these, too, follow a pattern. Try to identify patterns in the spelling of irregular verbs.

Unit 10: Suffixes – 'ment'

Objectives

- To revise word endings.
- To recognise and spell words containing the suffix 'ment'.

Spelling Focus

- A **suffix** is a group of letters we add to the **end** of a word.
- Suffixes **change the meaning** and the **purpose** of a word.
- They can sometimes change the **spelling** of a **root word**.
- The suffix 'ment' is quite common. It is often used to change a verb to a noun.

enjoy – enjoyment

The video game gave me a lot of enjoyment.

Starter

1. Copy the following words. Underline the root word and circle the suffix. The first one is done for you.

   (a) move(ment)
   (b) involvement
   (c) agreement
   (d) employment
   (e) amusement
   (f) improvement
   (g) management
   (h) argument

2. Divide the words into syllables like this: ***move + ment***.

3. The suffix 'ment' is often used to change a verb into a noun. Complete the examples in the chart to distinguish between these parts of speech.

Noun	Verb
involvement	*To involve*
agreement	
employment	
amusement	
improvement	
management	
argument	

Practice >>

4 Write these 'ment' words.
Write the root word from which each came.
Do it like this: ***entertainment – entertain***

- (a) amusement
- (b) astonishment
- (c) arrangement
- (d) government
- (e) development
- (f) disagreement
- (g) establishment
- (h) merriment

5 Split each word into syllables like this:
entertainment*: *en + ter + tain + ment

Extension >>>

6 Spell these words correctly.
Use a dictionary to help.

- (a) arguement
- (b) goverment
- (c) parlament
- (d) enviroment
- (e) advertisment
- (f) excitment
- (g) temparament
- (h) developement
- (i) assinment

REMEMBER

You need to be able to separate the root of a word from its suffix.

7 Invent mnemonics for each of the words to help you to spell them correctly.
For example: ***A GOVERNment GOVERNs.***

Feedback

The suffix 'ment' is often used to change a verb to a noun. Adding certain suffixes to words can change the spelling of the root word. In most cases, 'ment' does not change the spelling of the root word. When it does there is normally a common-sense reason.

Unit 11: Suffixes – 'ing' and 'ed'

Objectives

- To consolidate verb endings, including vowel suffixes.
- To spell regular verbs ending in the suffixes 'ing' and 'ed'.

Spelling Focus

- We can change many **verbs** into the **past tense** by adding the **suffixes 'ed'** and **'ing'**. Sometimes we do **not** have to **change** the **spelling** of the **root verb**.

  The teacher shouted at Tom.

  She was shouting very loudly.

- If a verb ends in 'e' we usually drop the 'e' and add 'ing' or 'ed'.

  Tom smiled at the teacher.

  He was smiling very sweetly.

- When you add 'ing' or 'ed' to single-syllable verbs where a final consonant is preceded by one vowel, the final consonant will double.

  The frog hopped onto the riverbank.

  The frog was hopping onto the riverbank when I saw him.

Starter

1 Copy and complete the chart.

Root verb	+ ing	+ ed
walk	*walking*	
call		
jump		
		climbed
	laughing	
look		
	kicking	
		sketched
open		
crash		

Practice >>

2 Add 'ing' and 'ed' to each of these verbs.

(a) rake (b) flame (c) gape (d) skate (e) save (f) glide (g) like (h) file (i) dine (j) dive

3 Write the root word of each of these verbs.
Do it like this: ***wiping = wipe + ing***

(a) stoned (b) hoping (c) joked (d) closing (e) voted (f) fuming (g) ruled (h) amusing (i) excused (j) tuning

Extension >>>

4 Copy the sentences below.
Choose the correct form of the verb in brackets to complete each sentence.

(a) The teacher _______ what he said. (believe)
(b) The sculptor was _______ a piece of wood. (shape)
(c) My friend _______ in a whisper. (answer)
(d) The athlete was just _______ her run. (complete)
(e) The sausages _______ in the pan. (sizzle)
(f) I didn't know what was _______. (happen)
(g) The girl was _______ about in the dark. (stumble)
(h) The musician _______ some lovely music. (compose)
(i) The baby was _______ an apple. (bite)
(j) My mum _______ my glass to the brim. (fill)

REMEMBER

If a single-syllable word ends in a consonant plus 'e' then we often drop the 'e' before adding the ending.

Feedback

When you add a suffix to the end of a word look carefully at the final letter of the root word.

Follow the rules like the ones in the Spelling Focus carefully.

When in doubt check, your spelling in a dictionary or with a computer spell check.

Unit 12: Ending in 'y'

Objectives

- To revise pluralisation and the modification of words ending in 'y'.
- To investigate and learn spelling rules.

Spelling Focus

- Sometimes, when you word build on to a word which ends in 'y', you may not be sure whether to change the final 'y' or keep it.

baby? babies? monkey? monkeys? shy? shyly?

- By working through the exercises in this unit, you should be able to come to some conclusions about this.

Starter

1. Write out the nouns below and their plurals. All the answers end in 's', but check your spelling in a dictionary.

   (a) one monkey, two monkeys
   (b) one lady, two ...
   (c) one berry, two ...
   (d) one country, two ...
   (e) one copy, two ...
   (f) one valley, two ...
   (g) one ruby, two ...
   (h) one key, two ...
   (i) one toy, two ...

2. Write a rule to explain how you make nouns ending in 'y' into the plural.

3. Look at the words in the box below.

   boy, baby, buoy, city, buy, cry, day, jelly, lorry, donkey, party, quay, try, tray, worry

   Sort the words into the two sections of this chart to help you to check your rule about plurals of nouns ending in 'y'. Does the rule work?

Vowel + y	Consonant + y

Practice >>

❹ Look at the box below.

carry, annoy, reply, stay, play, worry, dry, delay, marry, destroy, enjoy, copy

Copy and complete the chart using the verbs from the box. Check your spelling in a dictionary.

Verb	Last letter	Second to last letter	Add 'ed' to verb	Add 's' to verb
carry	*consonant*	*consonant*		

❺ Write a rule to explain whether the spelling of the verb changes or not when you add 'ed' or 's'.

Extension >>>

❻ Add 'ing' to these verbs:

apply, study, copy, bury, reply, cry

– and explain what happens.

❼ Add 'ly' to these adjectives:

happy, easy, lazy, heavy, pretty, steady

Check your spelling in a dictionary.
What happens?

❽ Add 'ing', 'd' and 's' to:

die, tie, lie

Check your spelling in a dictionary.
What happens?

REMEMBER

Learning the rules is helpful but also note that there may be many exceptions!

Feedback

It is good to learn rules about spelling. However, for every rule you will find exceptions.

The trick is to learn the rule but also note down any exceptions. Investigate the words that do not follow rules. Look carefully at the number of syllables, and the position of vowels and consonants.

Unit 13: Ending in 'e'

Objectives

- To revise word endings.
- To investigate and apply spelling rules.

Spelling Focus

- Sometimes, when you word build on to a word which ends in 'e', you may not be sure whether to drop the final 'e' or keep it.

caring? careful? loving? lovely?

- By working through the exercises in this unit, you should be able to come to some conclusions about this.
- Placing an 'e' on the end of a word can change its sound so you have to be careful before you remove it!
- Dealing with the final 'e' leads to some of the most common errors in spelling.

Starter

1. Add the suffix 'ing' to these words. Check your answers in a dictionary.

(a) write
(b) care
(c) ride
(d) hope
(e) love
(f) come
(g) believe
(h) delete

+ ing

2. Explain what you notice has happened to the spelling of these words when the suffix 'ing' is added.

3. Check whether your conclusions are correct by investigating the addition of suffixes to these words ending in 'e'. Use some suffixes that begin with a vowel and some that begin with a consonant. Use a dictionary.

cycle, fake, force, frame, free, hassle, programme, realise, rule, tackle, terrorise, wrestle

Practice >>

❹ Add the suffix 'full' to these words and check in a dictionary to see what happens to the final 'l' of the suffix.
Write the new word.

(a) hope
(b) care
(c) peace
+ full

❺ Add the suffix 'ly' to these words.
Write the new word.
Check your answers in a dictionary.

(a) safe
(b) love
(c) wise
(d) brave
+ ly

(e) lone
(f) active
(g) complete
(h) fortunate
+ ly

Extension >>>

❻ Copy and complete these rules to explain what you have discovered about adding suffixes to words ending in 'e'.
(a) When you add the suffix 'ing' to words ending in 'e' ...
(b) When you add the suffix 'ful' to words ending in 'e' ...
(c) When you add the suffix 'ly' to words ending in 'e' ...

❼ Find three more examples to illustrate each of these three rules.

❽ Find some exceptions to the rules. For example, see what happens when you add suffixes to these words.

tie, lie, die, probable, possible, terrible, single, simple

Check your answers in a dictionary.

Feedback

If you are adding the suffix 'ing' to words ending in 'e' then the 'e' is usually dropped.

If you are adding the suffixes 'ful' (remember – never a double 'l') or 'ly' to words ending in 'e' then the final 'e' remains unchanged.

Unit 14: Ending in 'tion' and 'sion'

Objective

- To consolidate the making of choices between similar endings.

Spelling Focus

- Two common **suffixes** are 'tion' and 'sion'.
- The letters 'tion' at the end of a word sound like 'shun'.

  Sam has a large collection of spiders.
- The letters 'sion' at the end of a word sound like 'zhun' when preceded by a vowel.

  There was a loud explosion.

Starter

1 Look at the words below.

protection	*collection*	*action*	*organisation*
creation	*direction*	*inspection*	
education	*generation*	*decoration*	

Copy the chart below. Sort the words in the box into the correct columns.

'-ction' words	'-ation' words

2 Write the root word from which each of the words comes. Do it like this: ***protection – protect***

3 (a) Find five words that end in 'sion', e.g. 'collision'.
(b) Find five words that end in 'ition', e.g. 'competition'.
(c) Find five words that end in 'otion', e.g. 'devotion'.
(d) Find five words that end in 'ution', e.g. 'constitution'.

Can you see anything that they have in common or that are different that might help you to spell them correctly?

Practice >>

❹ Copy and complete the chart.
Change each of the verbs into a noun using the correct suffix.

Verb	Noun
televise	television
decide	
include	
confuse	
provide	
explode	
divide	
erode	
deride	
invade	

REMEMBER

To spell words you need to listen to the sounds that different letters make.

Extension >>>

❺ Copy the words below. Choose 'tion' or 'sion' to complete each. Use a dictionary to help.

(a) imagina_____
(b) exhibi_____
(c) occa_____
(d) revi_____
(e) competi_____
(f) separa_____
(g) seclu_____
(h) cohe_____
(i) conversa_____
(j) ventila_____
(k) inci_____
(l) illu_____

❻ Think of mnemonics or rules which will help you to spell these words in future. For example:

I won a PET In the comPETItion.

❼ Think of five words that end in 'ssion'. Write them down. Can you work out any rules that can help you to differentiate these words from the others in this unit?

Feedback

The suffixes 'tion' and 'sion' sound very similar. Therefore you need to look at the words themselves and their derivation or function.

Unit 15: Phonemes

Objective

- To sound out words phonemically.

Spelling Focus

- A **phoneme** is the **smallest unit of sound** in a word.

  The word '***cat***' has three phonemes.

  c - a - t

  The word '***eyes***' has two phonemes.

  eye - s

- Sometimes the same phoneme can make a different sound in a word.

  r<u>oo</u>t bl<u>oo</u>d

Starter

1 Copy the chart.
Circle the letters which each word has in common.
Underline the word in each set which sounds different.

(a)	*marry*	*party*	*star*	*market*
(b)	*snowing*	*now*	*bowl*	*know*
(c)	*call*	*small*	*stall*	*shall*
(d)	*waste*	*ask*	*pass*	*disaster*
(e)	*pouring*	*hour*	*course*	*four*
(f)	*earth*	*early*	*dear*	*rehearse*

2 Discuss how this poem proves how difficult phonemes can be when learning how to spell.

A moth is not a moth in mother,
Nor both in bother, broth in brother,
And here is not a match for there
Nor dear and fear for bear and pear,
And then there's dose and rose and lose –
Just look them up – and goose and choose.

And cork and work and card and ward,
And font and front and work and sword,
And do and go and thwart and cart –
Come, come, I've hardly made a start!
A dreadful language? Man alive,
I'd mastered it when I was five.

Practice >>

3 Copy and complete the chart below. The first one has been done for you.

Phoneme	Example	Same sound	Same sound	Different sound
'ea'	*meat*	*seat*	*beat*	*bear*
'oa'	*float*			
'oo'	*soon*			
'ai'	*pain*			
'ou'	*round*			
'ie'	*field*			

4 Use a word from each box in a sentence.

Extension >>>

5 In each box, add five words which contain the underlined phoneme and make the same sound. Remember these do not have to be spelled the same. For example, under 'oe' you could write '*two*' and '*through*'.

shoe	*could*	*stay*
dirty	*horse*	*cloud*

6 Use a word from each box in a sentence.

REMEMBER

Being able to look at and identify phonemes in words is a valuable way of learning how to spell.

Feedback

You should be able to break down words into their phonemes and look at the variety of letters that may be used to create the same sound.

Unit 16: Syllables

Objective

- To sound out and build up spellings by syllabic parts.

Spelling Focus

- **Longer words** can be **broken down** into **smaller parts** called **syllables**.

  Bad has one syllable.
  Bad/min/ton has three syllables.
- Each syllable must contain **at least one vowel**.
- Syllables do not have to make whole words by themselves.
- Breaking words into syllables is a good way to see how words are built up.
- You can also construct new words from separate syllables.

Starter

1 Write out the words which are the answers to these syllable sums. Write the number of syllables in each word in brackets:
birth + day = birthday (2)

(a) chil + dren =
(b) swim + ming =
(c) veg + et + a + ble =
(d) fol + low + ing =
(e) an + im + als =
(f) nec + es + sar + y =
(g) bi + cy + cle =
(h) im + por + tant =
(i) bal + loon =
(j) com + for + ta + ble =
(k) dan + ger + ous =

2 Words can be built up into 'word families'. Divide these words into syllables and explain what each family has in common.

signal *signalman* *signatory* *signature* *significance* *signify* *significant*	*likely* *likeable* *likelihood* *liken* *likeness* *likewise* *liking*
friendly *friendship* *friendliness* *friendless* *friendship*	*scripture* *description* *prescription* *manuscript* *postscript*

Practice >>

3 Copy and complete the chart. Make three-syllable words.

	1st syllable	2nd syllable	3rd syllable	Complete word
a	*sig*	*ledge*	*ine*	*signature*
b	*know*	*nat*	*ion*	
c	*med*	*pic*	*ic*	
d	*sus*	*fic*	*ite*	
e	*rel*	*all*	*ient*	
f	*met*	*at*	*ive*	
g	*de*	*ease*	*ure*	
h	*dis*	*fin*	*able*	
i	*ef*	*ic*	*ed*	

4 Explain how knowing how to spell the similar words below can make spelling the words above easier.

sign, know, medical, suspect, relate, metal, finite, ease, effect

Extension >>>

5 How many syllables are there in each of the words in the box?

temperature	*February*	*analysis*	*environment*
gnome	*received*	*laboratory*	*medieval*
interesting	*circumference*	*population*	*conscientiously*
description	*alliteration*	*growth*	
decided	*investigation*	*volcanic*	

Copy and complete the chart by writing the correct words in the appropriate column.

1 syllable	2 syllables	3 syllables	4 syllables	5 syllables	6 syllables

Feedback

Splitting words into their constituent parts is valuable in learning how to spell. Each syllable should have at least one vowel.

Another useful spelling strategy is finding words within words. For example: 'sign' is a word in 'signature' even though the words sound very different.

Unit 17: Roots

Objectives

- To draw on analogies to known words.
- To investigate the relationship between origins and meanings.

Spelling Focus

- Sometimes a number of words will come from the **same root**.

  helpful

  helpless

  helper

  unhelpful

- **Prefixes** and **suffixes** may be added to **change the meaning** and **function** of the word.
- Root words can also be helpful because they may come from other languages. If you know what the root word means, this can help you to understand the meaning of related words.

  '***Signum***' is the Latin word for a '***mark***'. You can find this root in such words as:

  sign

  signal

  signature

Starter

1 Copy this chart.
Circle the common root words in each row.
The first one is done for you.

knowing	unknown	knowledge
advent	invent	prevent
pressing	depress	pressure
marked	marks	remarkable
disagree	agreeable	agreement
clearly	clearance	unclear
cheaply	cheapen	cheaper
photograph	telegraph	autograph

2 Use a dictionary to find out what these roots mean.
An etymological dictionary would be most useful.

Practice >>

3 Many words have Latin roots. Look at the words below.

verbal	*inscribe*	*sign*	*signal*	*detract*
spectator	*proverb*	*subtract*	*manuscript*	*spectacles*

Copy and complete the chart with examples from the word box. Use a dictionary to help. The first example has been done for you.

Latin word	Meaning	English words derived from it
signum	*mark*	*sign, signal*
specto	*I look*	
tractum	*drawn away*	
scribo	*I write*	
verbum	*word*	

4 Find one more example for each column of the chart. Use a dictionary to help.

Extension >>>

5 Here are some more Latin roots, meanings and one English word which comes from each. Copy and complete the chart with more English words from the same root. Include as many English words as possible.

Latin word	Meaning	English words from the root
positum	*placed*	*deposit*
pendeo	*I hang*	*suspend*
terra	*land*	*terrace*
primus	*first*	*prime*
annus	*year*	*annual*
civis	*citizen*	*civic*
fortis	*strong*	*fortify*

Feedback

Many root words come from Latin or Greek. You need to be able to identify the roots of words but also be able to see what happens when we add a prefix or a suffix – or both – to the root word.

Unit 18: Compound words

Objectives

- To draw on analogies and familiar spelling patterns.
- To investigate compound words.

Spelling Focus

- A **compound word** is a word which is made up of **two smaller words**.

  hand + bag = handbag

  cup + board = cupboard

- Take care! We don't always pronounce the words as they are spelled.

Starter

1 Match each word in Set A with a word in Set B to make a compound word.

Set A	Set B	
birth →	brush	
under	ever	
hand	ground	
tooth	day →	birthday
time	bow	
when	bag	
wall	hole	
key	about	
rain	table	
round	paper	

Practice >>

2 Copy these compound words. Break them into their two smaller words. Do it like this: ***butter + fly = butterfly.***

- (a) breakfast
- (b) cupboard
- (c) eyesight
- (d) grandmother
- (e) motorway
- (f) postcard
- (g) bookworm
- (h) hedgehog
- (i) toothache
- (j) bombshell
- (k) dustbin
- (l) waistcoat

3 Choose any five of these compound words and explain how they developed their meanings by combining two separate nouns.
For example: ***break + fast = breakfast***
This was the first meal of the day so literally people broke their fast (the period in which they did not eat).
An etymological dictionary might help.

Extension >>>

4 Think of a suitable word to complete each compound word.

- (a) ____ fall
- (b) ____ paper
- (c) ____ step
- (d) ____ roads
- (e) ____ cloth
- (f) ____ berry
- (g) ____ work
- (h) ____ table
- (i) ____ way

REMEMBER

Splitting words into their smaller parts is a valuable strategy in learning how to spell.

5 Think of at least three compound words beginning with each of these words.

- (a) foot
- (b) some
- (c) any
- (d) moon
- (e) fire
- (f) tea
- (g) back
- (h) post
- (i) tooth
- (j) over
- (k) hand
- (l) hair

Feedback

Knowledge of compound words will help you in splitting and combining some words.

Another useful strategy is finding words within words. For example, 'cup' is a word in 'cupboard' even though the words sound very different.

Unit 19: Derivation

Objectives

- To revise work on etymology.
- To extend work on origins and derivations.

Spelling Focus

- We can understand why many words are spelled in a particular way if we can understand their **origin** and **derivation** (where they came from originally).

  Telephone comes from two Greek words.

  '***Tele***' means '***from afar***', '***phone***' means '***sound***'.

- Knowing these Greek prefixes and roots now helps us to understand the meaning of the word. It also helps us spell other words.

  Television means being able to see from afar.

Starter

1. Each word in Column A is to do with a particular number. Using a dictionary, match each word with a number in Column B. Write each word with its number.
uniform – ***uni*** (one).

Column A	Column B
uniform	*one*
triangle	*two*
decimal	*three*
quarter	*four*
century	*five*
millennium	*eight*
octet	*ten*
bicycle	*one hundred*
pentagon	*one thousand*
unique	

Practice >>

❷ Copy and complete the chart. Use your dictionary.

Prefix	Meaning	Two examples using the prefix
mono		
sub		*subway*
dis		
trans	*across*	
poly	*many*	
anti		
auto		*automatic*
circum		
tele		

Extension >>>

❸ Make your own dictionary using these new words.

- Write a definition for each word or phrase.
- Write where you think the words might be derived from.

Many of these words are new to our language and might not yet be in your dictionary.

ⓐ wheelie
ⓑ backing track
ⓒ nerd
ⓓ disc jockey
ⓔ one-armed bandit
ⓕ self-service
ⓖ comprehensive school
ⓗ trailer
ⓘ bucket shop
ⓙ teenager
ⓚ mail order
ⓛ play station
ⓜ developing country

Feedback

Words have developed over time from various languages. Knowing root words can be helpful in remembering how to spell words.

You need to be able to identify the roots of words but also be able to see what happens when we add a prefix or a suffix – or both – to the root word.

Unit 20: Patterns – 'i' before 'e'

Objective

- To investigate and apply spelling rules.

Spelling Focus

- When you spell a word containing the 'ee' sound, you may not be sure whether to put 'ei' or 'ie'.

relief?

receive?

By working through the exercises in this unit, you should be able to come to some conclusions about this.

Starter

1 One word in each pair below is spelled incorrectly.
Use your dictionary to check the spelling.
Write the correct word.

- (a) chief, freind
- (b) handkercheif, ceiling
- (c) theif, field
- (d) Kieth, perceive
- (e) seige, priest
- (f) hieght, deceiver
- (g) queit, seize

2 Brainstorm a list of words in which 'i' and 'e' are next to each other – in any order.
Look for patterns in the letters before and after and the sound they make.

Practice >>

❸ Put 'ie' or 'ei' into the following words. Use a dictionary. Write out the correct words.

ⓐ bel _ _ ve
ⓑ y _ _ ld
ⓒ gr _ _ f
ⓓ rec _ _ ve
ⓔ br _ _ f
ⓕ ach _ _ ve
ⓖ dec _ _ ve
ⓗ gr _ _ ving
ⓘ conc _ _ ve
ⓙ p _ _ ce
ⓚ sh _ _ ld
ⓛ rel _ _ f
ⓜ dec _ _ t
ⓝ p _ _ r
ⓞ s _ _ ge
ⓟ rec _ _ pt
ⓠ conc _ _ t
ⓡ n _ _ ce

❹ Copy and complete the chart using the words above. What sound does the 'ie' or 'ei' make in all these words?

Words containing 'ie'	Letter before 'ie'	Words containing 'ei'	Letter before 'ei'
piece	*p*		

Extension >>>

❺ Copy and complete the following rule.
Look closely at the letter which comes before 'ie' or 'ei'.

'I' before __ except after __ when it makes the sound __.

❻ Write four more words which prove your rule.

❼ Use your dictionary. Find five exceptions to the rule, e.g. ***seize***.

❽ Write sentences using the five exceptions you have found.

REMEMBER

Like most rules the 'i' before 'e' rule has many exceptions and these have to be noted and learned.

Feedback

Everyone seems to know this 'rule' ('i' before 'e' except after 'c' when it sounds like 'ee') but it still causes real problems in spelling. Knowing the rule should make you stop at words making the sound and see if it applies.

Unit 21: Mnemonics

Objectives

- To learn words on sight and memorise critical features.
- To invent and use mnemonics for irregular or difficult spellings.

Spelling Focus

- **Mnemonics** are ways we **invent** to **help us remember** something.
- Mnemonics are very helpful when you are trying to remember how to spell tricky words.

Wasps Always Sting

spells *WAS*.

Rhythm Has Your Toes Hopping Mad

spells *RHYTHM*.

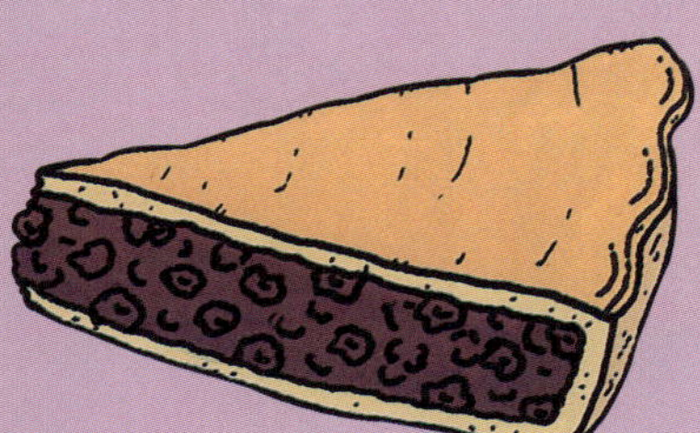

Starter

1. Match the mnemonic to the word it will help you to spell. Write them out. Look for the clues – the capital letters can be found in the words.

Mnemonics	Words
(a) *It caused me ANGER. I'm …*	*teacher*
(b) *I like PIE. Give me a …*	*government*
(c) *He ATE it all. My …*	*temperature*
(d) *There's a RAT in …*	*chocolate*
(e) *They GOVERN.*	*piece*
(f) *They're a pain. They contain an ACHE.*	*dangerous*

Practice >>

❷ Write mnemonics to help you spell these words. Write your words on the lines, starting with the appropriate letter of the original word.

F	m	t	W
e	i	w	e
b	n	e	d
r	i	l	n
u	a	f	e
a	t	t	s
r	u	h	d
y	r		a
	e		y

❸ Check the derivation of the four words above in a dictionary to help you remember them. For example, the prefix in miniature is 'mini', meaning small.

Extension >>>

❹ Write out these words. Look for smaller words in each word and underline them.

Use these to write mnemonics that will help you remember the word.

is<u>land</u>	together
wonderful	geography
height	practice
ghost	juice
vegetable	because

REMEMBER

There is no one way of remembering how to spell a word.

Feedback

Mnemonics are very personal. We all think differently and remember certain things in certain ways.

This is why the best mnemonics are those made up by yourself. Someone else may not understand them but if it enables you to spell the word, there is no problem!

Unit 22: Dictionaries

Objective

- To use dictionaries to discover meanings of abbreviations and acronyms.

Spelling Focus

- Dictionaries can help you to find out what **abbreviations** mean.
- Abbreviations are **shortened forms** of words or phrases; for example, ***RSVP*** at the bottom of an invitation is a request for you to reply.
- Dictionaries can also tell you how these abbreviations were **derived**:

  RSVP is the shortened version of the French expression, ***Répondez-vous s'il vous plait***.
- **Acronyms** are abbreviations, but are whole words formed from the first letters of other words:

  The word radar comes from RAdio Detection And Ranging.
- Besides telling you the meaning of a word, a dictionary is useful for checking spelling – but take care because not all words will be in a dictionary.

Starter

1 Use a dictionary.
Write these abbreviations in full.

(a) i.o.u.
(b) m.p.h.
(c) Anon.
(d) B.C.
(e) A.D.
(f) B.B.C.
(g) S.O.S.
(h) U.S.A.
(i) R.S.P.C.A.

2 Use a dictionary.
Explain the derivation and meaning of these abbreviations.

(a) o'clock
(b) Hallowe'en
(c) p.m.
(d) a.m.

Practice >>

3 Copy this note, writing all the abbreviations (where appropriate) in full.

> Mr and Mrs Nagenda live in Peace St. close to the Elland Rd. football stadium. It is two km. from Trafalgar Sq. and opposite the pk. They will meet us on Sat. morn. or Sun. aft.
>
> Mr and Mrs Nagenda own their own business – Nagenda and Co. Ltd. I am in charge of the art dept.
>
> See you soon.
>
> Ray
>
> P.S. Forgot to ask you to bring some food, etc.
>
> P.T.O. Plse call if there is a problem.

4 What do you notice about the punctuation necessary when you use abbreviations?

5 Check in your dictionary to find the derivation of Mr, Mrs, etc. and P.S.

6 Use a dictionary to find out the origin of these acronyms.

(a) ROM (b) NAAFI (c) WRENS

Extension >>>

7 Copy and complete the chart.
Use your dictionary and other reference sources to find the original words.

Shortened word	Original longer word(s)	Parts missed out
bus	*omnibus*	*omni*
phone		
mac		
plane		
pram		
fridge		
photo		
amps		
piano		
perm		

Feedback

Dictionaries are essential reference sources and you need to be able to find your way around dictionaries as speedily and efficiently as possible. Use the header words at the top of the pages to help you.

Unit 23: Etymology

Objective

- To understand the function of an etymological dictionary.

Spelling Focus

- An **etymological dictionary** is one that tells you about the **origins** of words. Look at the extract below. 'Etymology' comes from an Ancient Greek word meaning 'the true sense of a word': ***etumon*** – true, ***logia*** – of words.

> **alphabet** / named after the first two Greek letters: *Alpha*, *Beta*; it originally meant the set of letters used in writing the Greek language; now it refers to any set of letters representing the simple sounds of language.
>
> **biscuit** / from Latin: *bis* (twice) *coctus* (cooked); to keep them fresh, biscuits used to be baked twice to make them hard.
>
> **dandelion** / from the French: *dent de lion* (lion's tooth), it describes the jagged edges of the leaves.
>
> **nickname** / from Anglo-Saxon: *ekename*, *eke* means *also*; a name that substitutes for the proper name of a person.

Starter

1 Read the information in the Spelling Focus section again. Answer these questions.

(a) What is an etymological dictionary?
(b) How is the word 'etymology' derived?
(c) From which language does 'alphabet' originally come?
(d) From which two words does 'alphabet' come?
(e) Explain how the word 'biscuit' came to be invented.
(f) From which language does 'dandelion' come?
(g) How did the plant get this name?
(h) From which language does 'nickname' come?
(i) How is it linked with the word 'also'?

Practice >>

2 Use a dictionary to find where these words originally came from.

microphone	*caravan*	*physics*	*bazaar*	*cot*
dungarees	*theology*	*kiosk*	*pyjamas*	*pharmacy*
automatic	*bungalow*	*thug*	*turban*	*lilac*

Sort them into the chart.

Words from Persian	Words from Greek	Words from Hindi
caravan		

3 Write sentences using any two words from each column.

Extension >>>

4 Research how these words came into our language. Look at the clues in the box.

(a) juggernaut
(b) marathon
(c) teddy bear
(d) macintosh
(e) hooligan
(f) sandwich

Clues

- Ancient Greek battle story,
- US president who refused to kill animal,
- Huge Hindu statue dragged through streets every year,
- Scot who invented waterproof material,
- Nineteenth-century Irish family in London known to be disorderly,
- Earl who invented a snack so that he would not have to stop playing cards.

REMEMBER

You can find information about the history and derivation of words in an etymological dictionary.

Feedback

Looking at derivation can show us how words are made up of smaller parts – words within words – or can give us clues and understanding of how words developed.

You need to be able to identify the root word, but also to see how adding a prefix or a suffix – or both – to the root affects the spelling of the root word.

Unit 24: Homophones

Objectives

- To secure the spelling of high frequency words.
- To distinguish between the spelling and meanings of common homophones.

Spelling Focus

- **Homophones** are words that **sound alike** but have **different meanings** or **spellings**.
- To be able to distinguish between homophones you need to be aware of the **context** in which the word is being used. Think about the confusion and the humour created in the example below from *Alice in Wonderland*.

  'Mine is a long and sad tale!' said the mouse, turning to Alice and sighing.

  'It is a long tail, certainly,' said Alice, looking down in wonder at the mouse's tail. 'But why do you call it sad?'

- Some homophones have more than one word that sounds like them.

That poor dog. He's got a thorn in his paw. Pour him a drink.

Starter

1. Match up the pairs of homophones in Set A and Set B.

Set A	Set B
bare	blue
dear	made
blew	bear
groan	deer
maid	grown
right	sun
son	flour
wood	write
wait	weight
flower	would

2. Explain the difference between these commonly confused homophones.

   (a) it's – its (b) there – their – they're

Practice >>

3 Copy each sentence. Choose the correct word to complete it. Use a dictionary, if necessary.

- (a) The _____ took off from the runway. (plane/plain)
- (b) We had to _____ out our wet clothes.
- (c) It was a _____ of time trying to find it.
- (d) The athlete strained a _____.
- (e) May I have a _____ of cake?
- (f) The children lost _____ way.
- (g) Don't eat _____ much.
- (h) We waited an _____ for _____ meal.

4 Write sentences to show you understand the difference between these commonly confused homophones.

(a) whose – who's (b) to – too – two (c) past – passed

Extension >>>

5 Rewrite each sentence. Use a correct word in place of the misspelled word.

- (a) The old man had little **hare** left on his head.
- (b) The thief had nerves of **steal**.
- (c) The **cereal** on television was great.
- (d) The footballer committed a **fowl**.
- (e) I ate a **current** bun.
- (f) The horse had a long **main**.
- (g) The soldier won a **meddle** for bravery.
- (h) Do you **peal** an apple before eating it?

6 Write a homophone for each of these.

- (a) boy
- (b) night
- (c) none
- (d) fair
- (e) key
- (f) root
- (g) hole
- (h) stake
- (i) seen
- (j) feet

REMEMBER

Homophones are words that sound alike but have different meanings or spellings.

Feedback

English has many words that sound exactly the same and can only be distinguished when placed in a particular context or when we see them written down. Spelling is therefore very important as it ensures that meaning is clear.

Unit 25: Common spelling errors

Objective

- To consolidate and secure the spellings of high-frequency words.

Spelling Focus

- This unit will highlight a variety of **strategies** to help you to spell difficult words. These include:
  - looking for **prefixes** and **word roots** that will help you to investigate the **derivation** of the word
  - breaking the words into **syllables** and pronouncing each part
  - identifying **smaller words** in larger words
  - inventing **mnemonics** from the words
  - using the Look, Say, Cover, Write, Check spelling strategy.

Starter

1 Look at the commonly misspelled words in the Problem Box.

Problem Box

accommodation	*interesting*	*February*
believe	*possession*	*miscellaneous*
concentration	*alcohol*	*necessary*
listening	*caught*	*permanent*
marriage	*continuous*	*remember*

Break the words into syllables and pronounce each part. Copy and complete the chart. Rewrite the word using the Look, Say, Cover, Write, Check spelling strategy.

Words	Syllables				
	1	2	3	4	5
accommodation	*ac*	*com*	*mo*	*da*	*tion*
believe					
concentration					

Practice >>

❷ Read the words in the box below.

beginning, business, conscience, environment, height, knowledge, outrageous, separate, government, queue, research strategy, weight

Look for small words in larger words. Copy and complete the chart. Rewrite the word using the Look, Say, Cover, Write, Check spelling strategy.

Word	Smaller words I have found
business	*bus, in, sin*
beginning	
conscience	

❸ Make mnemonics from the words you find. These can help you to remember the spelling of words.

I will take the BUS IN to get to my BUSINess.

Extension >>>

❹ Consider the words in the box.

beautiful	*physical*	*audible*	*surprise*
interrupt	*technology*	*disappear*	*technique*
signature	*tomorrow*	*questionnaire*	*Wednesday*
description	*women*	*Saturday*	

Look for prefixes, suffixes or roots that will help you with the derivation of the word. Use a dictionary. An etymological dictionary will be helpful. Copy and complete the chart. Rewrite the word using Look, Say, Cover, Write, Check.

Words	Prefix, suffix or root	Derivation	Other words I have found
beautiful	*beau*	*French for beautiful*	
interrupt			
signature			

❺ Find other words which use the same prefix, suffix or root as the words above.

Feedback

Everyone learns in a different way. What works for you is what matters. Think about which of these strategies **you** find useful.

Unit 26: Art words

Objective

- To consolidate and secure the spellings and meanings of subject-specific key words.

Spelling Focus

- Many words in **Art** come from **ancient times** and from cultures such as **Italy** where Art was considered to be very important.
- Many subjects use **technical vocabulary.** These subject-specific words are important for an accurate understanding of the subject.
- This unit will highlight a **variety of strategies** to help you to spell and understand these words. These include:
  - looking for **prefixes** and **word roots** that will help you to investigate the **derivation** of the word
  - breaking the words into **syllables** and pronouncing each part
  - identifying **smaller words** in larger words
  - inventing **mnemonics** from the words
  - using the Look, Say, Cover, Write, Check spelling strategy.

Starter

1 Look at the commonly misspelled words in the Problem Box.

Problem Box

abstract	*colour*	*kiln*
acrylic	*dimension*	*sketch*
perspective	*frieze*	*impressionism*
collage	*portrait*	*sculpture*

Break the words into syllables and pronounce each part.
Copy and complete the chart.
Rewrite the word using the Look, Say, Cover, Write, Check spelling strategy.

Words	Syllables			
	1	2	3	4
abstract	*ab*	*stract*		
acrylic				
perspective				

Practice >>

❷ Read the words in the box below.

charcoal, collection, crosshatch, display, exhibition, highlight, landscape, perspective, movement, criticism, mannerism, proportion

Look for small words in larger words. Copy and complete the chart. Rewrite each word using the Look, Say, Cover, Write, Check spelling strategy.

Words	Smaller words I have found
charcoal	*arc, coal*
collection	
crosshatch	

❸ Make mnemonics from the words you find. These can help you to remember the spelling of words.

CharCOAL is as black as COAL.

Extension >>>

❹ Consider the words in the box.

spectrum	*gallery*	*Renaissance*	*naturalism*
palette	*easel*	*Baroque*	*pastel*
illusion	*foreground*	*fresco*	*photography*

Look for prefixes, suffixes or roots that will help you with the derivation of the word. Use a dictionary. An etymological dictionary will be helpful. Copy and complete the chart. Rewrite the word using the Look, Say, Cover, Write, Check spelling strategy.

Words	Prefix, suffix or root	Derivation	Other words I have found
spectrum		*Latin – to do with looking*	
palette			
illusion			

❺ Find other words which use the same prefix, suffix or root as the words above.

Feedback

Everyone learns subject-specific words in a different way. Think about which of these strategies **you** find useful when spelling difficult words in Art:

- the sound of a word
- the pattern a word makes
- making up a rhyme or a mnemonic.

Unit 27: Technology words

Objective

- To consolidate and secure the spellings and meanings of subject-specific key words.

Spelling Focus

- **Technology** uses many **specialised** words. Some are very new and are linked to modern machines and equipment. Other Technology words are very **old** and are linked to ancient skills of working in metal and wood.
- This unit will highlight a variety of strategies to help you to spell and understand these words. These include:
  - looking for prefixes and word roots that will help you to investigate the derivation of the word
  - breaking the words into syllables and pronouncing each part
  - identifying smaller words in larger words
  - inventing mnemonics from the words
  - using the Look, Say, Cover, Write, Check spelling strategy.

Starter

1 Look at the commonly misspelled words in the Problem Box.

Problem Box

aesthetic	*fibre*	*production*
component	*flowchart*	*recipe*
diet	*mineral*	*vitamin*
plastic	*presentation*	

Break the words into syllables and pronounce each part. Copy and complete the chart. Rewrite the word using the Look, Say, Cover, Write, Check spelling strategy.

Words	Syllables			
	1	2	3	4
aesthetic	*aes*	*thet*	*ic*	
component				
diet				

Practice >>

❷ Read the words in the box below.

disassemble, flour, hygiene, ingredient, machine, malnutrition, protein, specification, weight, temperature

Look for small words in larger words. Copy and complete the chart. Rewrite each word using the Look, Say, Cover, Write, Check spelling strategy.

Words	Smaller words I have found
disassemble	*dis, ass*
flour	
malnutrition	

❸ Make mnemonics from the words you find. These can help you to remember the spelling of words.

There's a NUT in malNUTrition.

Extension >>>

❹ Consider the words in the box.

technology carbohydrate design evaluation fabric innovation linen manufacture portfolio textile polyester

Look for prefixes, suffixes or roots that will help you with the derivation of the word. Use a dictionary. An etymological dictionary will be helpful. Copy and complete the chart. Rewrite the word using the Look, Say, Cover, Write, Check spelling strategy.

Words	Prefix, suffix or root	Derivation	Other words I have found
technology	*techno*	*'Technicus' (Latin) and 'Technikos' (Greek) means art or craft*	
carbohydrate			
design			

❺ Find other words which use the same prefix, suffix or root as the words above.

Feedback

Think about which of these strategies **you** find useful when spelling difficult words in Technology:

- making up a rhyme or a mnemonic
- breaking words up into their constituent parts and identify words inside them
- knowing where a word is derived from.

Unit 28: Drama words

Objective

- To consolidate and secure the spellings and meanings of subject-specific key words.

Spelling Focus

- Many words in **Drama** come from the ancient world as Drama was an important art form in ancient Greece and Rome. However, Drama has changed and an entirely **new vocabulary** is now associated with it.
- This unit will highlight a variety of strategies to help you to spell and understand these words. These include:
  - looking for prefixes and word roots that will help you to investigate the derivation of the word
  - breaking the words into syllables and pronouncing each part
  - identifying smaller words in larger words
  - inventing mnemonics from the words
  - using the Look, Say, Cover, Write, Check spelling strategy.

Starter

1. Look at the commonly misspelled words in the Problem Box.

Problem Box

improvisation	*performance*	*narrator*
character	*playwright*	*theatre*
costume	*role*	*producer*
director	*dialogue*	*Shakespearean*

Break the words into syllables and pronounce each part. Copy and complete the chart. Rewrite the word using the Look, Say, Cover, Write, Check spelling strategy.

Words	Syllables				
	1	2	3	4	5
improvisation	*im*	*pro*	*vi*	*sa*	*tion*
character					
costume					

Practice >>

❷ Read the words in the box below.

characteristics, curtain, dramatise, entrance, freeze, inspire, movement, position, spotlight, theatrical

Look for small words in larger words. Copy and complete the chart. Rewrite each word using the Look, Say, Cover, Write, Check spelling strategy.

Words	Smaller words I have found
characteristics	*character, act,*
curtain	
dramatise	

❸ Make mnemonics from the words you find. These can help you to remember the spelling of words.

You can ACT in charACTer to show your CHARACTERistics.

Extension >>>

❹ Consider the words in the box.

scene	*costume*	*opera*
scenario	*applause*	*ovation*
rehearsal	*audience*	*proscenium*
exit	*script*	

Look for prefixes, suffixes or roots that will help you with the derivation of the word. Use a dictionary. An etymological dictionary will be helpful. Copy and complete the chart. Rewrite the word using the Look, Say, Cover, Write, Check spelling strategy.

Words	Prefix, suffix or root	Derivation	Other words I have found
scene	*scene*	*Latin – 'scena': a stage*	
scenario			
rehearsal			

❺ Find other words which use the same prefix, suffix or root as the words above.

REMEMBER

Everyone learns subject-specific words in a different way.

Feedback

Think about which of these strategies **you** find useful when spelling difficult words in Drama:

- the sound of a word
- the pattern a word makes
- making up a rhyme or a mnemonic.

Unit 29: English words

Objective

- To consolidate and secure the spellings and meanings of subject-specific key words.

Spelling Focus

- **English** as a subject is not just about our language. It also deals with the study of **literature** and our responses to it. Much of this language was originally developed in **ancient times** when literature was seen as one of the greatest art forms.
- This unit will highlight a variety of strategies to help you to spell and understand these words. These include:
  - looking for prefixes and word roots that will help you to investigate the derivation of the word
  - breaking the words into syllables and pronouncing each part
  - identifying smaller words in larger words
  - inventing mnemonics from the words
  - using the Look, Say, Cover, Write, Check spelling strategy.

Starter

1. Look at the commonly misspelled words in the Problem Box.

Problem Box

advertisement	*consonant*	*pamphlet*
alliteration	*exclamation*	*resolution*
comma	*grammar*	*vocabulary*
comparison	*narrative*	

Break the words into syllables and pronounce each part. Copy and complete the chart. Rewrite the word using the Look, Say, Cover, Write, Check spelling strategy.

Words	Syllables				
	1	2	3	4	5
advertisement	*ad*	*ver*	*tise*	*ment*	
alliteration					
comma					

Practice >>

❷ Read the words in the box below.

personification, simile, atmosphere, clause, conjunction, expression, figurative, imagery, paragraph, vowel, subordinate, rhyme

Look for small words in larger words. Copy and complete the chart. Rewrite each word using the Look, Say, Cover, Write, Check spelling strategy.

Words	Smaller words I have found
personification	*person, son, if, cat*
simile	
atmosphere	

❸ Make mnemonics from the words you find. These can help you to remember the spelling of words.

You need a PERSON and a CAT for PERSONifiCATion.

Extension >>>

❹ Consider the words in the box.

scene	*cliché*	*preposition*
apostrophe	*dialogue*	*subordinate*
metaphor	*soliloquy*	*suffix*
onomatopoeia	*genre*	*tabloid*
chorus	*prefix*	

REMEMBER

There are many ways to learn correct spellings. What works for you is what matters.

Look for prefixes, suffixes or roots that will help you with the derivation of the word. Use a dictionary. An etymological dictionary will be helpful. Copy and complete the chart. Rewrite the word using the Look, Say, Cover, Write, Check spelling strategy.

Words	Prefix, suffix or root	Derivation	Other words I have found
apostrophe	*apostrophe*	*Greek – 'apostrophe': a turning away*	

❺ Find other words which use the same prefix, suffix or root as the words above.

Feedback

Think about which of these **you** find useful when spelling difficult words in English:

- making up a rhyme or a mnemonic
- breaking words up into their constituent parts and identify words inside them
- knowing where a word is derived from.

Unit 30: Geography words

Objective

- To consolidate and secure the spellings and meanings of subject-specific key words.

Spelling Focus

- Words in **Geography** often seem **long** and **complicated**. This is because they have been developed to describe complicated and often **scientific processes**. Many of the words were coined in the past, so knowing the **derivation** of the words is especially useful.
- This unit will highlight a variety of strategies to help you to spell and understand these words. These include:
  - looking for prefixes and word roots that will help you to investigate the derivation of the word
  - breaking the words into syllables and pronouncing each part
  - identifying smaller words in larger words
  - inventing mnemonics from the words
  - using the Look, Say, Cover, Write, Check spelling strategy.

Starter

1 Look at the commonly misspelled words in the Problem Box.

Problem Box

population	*employment*	*tourist*
erosion	*longitude*	*transportation*
growth	*pollution*	*estuary*
mountainous	*rural*	
contour	*situation*	

Break the words into syllables and pronounce each part. Copy and complete the chart. Rewrite the word using the Look, Say, Cover, Write, Check spelling strategy.

Words	Syllables			
	1	2	3	4
population	*pop*	*u*	*la*	*tion*
erosion				
growth				

Practice >>

❷ Read the words in the box below.

temperature, climate, vegetation, abroad, desert, country, habitat, landscape, latitude, national, provision, settlement, weather

Look for small words in larger words. Copy and complete the chart. Rewrite each word using the Look, Say, Cover, Write, Check spelling strategy.

Words	Smaller words I have found
temperature	*temper, rat*
climate	

❸ Make mnemonics from the words you find. These can help you to remember the spelling of words.

There's a hot TEMPER in TEMPERature.

Extension >>>

❹ Consider the words in the box.

urban	*infrastructure*	*transport*	*thermometer*
authority	*international*	*cyclone*	*atlas*
climate	*physical*	*equator*	

Look for prefixes, suffixes or roots that will help you with the derivation of the word. Use a dictionary. An etymological dictionary will be helpful. Copy and complete the chart. Rewrite the word using the Look, Say, Cover, Write, Check spelling strategy.

Word	Prefix, suffix or root	Derivation	Other words I have found
urban	*urban*	*Latin – 'urbanus': relating to a city/town*	

❺ Find other words which use the same prefix, suffix or root as the words above.

Feedback

Think about which of these strategies **you** find useful when spelling difficult words in Geography:

- the pattern a word makes
- making up a rhyme or a mnemonic.
- breaking words up into their constituent parts and identify words inside them

Published by Letts Educational
The Chiswick Centre
414 Chiswick High Road
London W4 5TF
Tel: 020 89963333
Fax: 020 87428390
email: mail@lettsed.co.uk
website: www.letts-education.com

Letts Educational Limited is a division of Granada Learning Limited, part of the Granada Media Group.

First published 2002
ISBN 1 84085 664 5

British Library Cataloguing in Publication Data
A catalogue record for this book is available from the British Library.

Acknowledgements

The publishers would like to thank the following for permission to use copyright material. Every effort has been made to trace copyright holders and to obtain their permission for the use of copyright material. The author and publishers will gladly receive information enabling them to rectify any error or omission in subsequent editions.

Illustrations: The British Library/Heritage-Images page 50; Topham Picturepoint pages 52, 54, 56, 58 and 62

Commissioned by Helen Clark
Project management by Vicky Butt and Aetos Ltd
Editing by Diana Roberts and Jane Otto
Cover design by Bigtop Design
Internal design by Aetos Ltd
Illustrations by Sylvie Poggio Artists Agency: Nick Duffy, Tony Forbes and Roger Langridge
Production by PDQ
Printed in the UK by Ashford Colour Press